EARLY CIVILIZATIONS

# Ancient Egypt

## BY KATHLEEN W. DEADY

Consultant:
Alexandra A. O'Brien, Ph.D.
Egyptologist
University of Chicago
Chicago, Illinois

Capstone
press

Mankato, Minnesota

Capstone Press
151 Good Counsel Drive • P.O. Box 669 • Mankato, Minnesota 56002
*www.capstonepress.com*

1 2 3 4 5 6 09 08 07 06 05 04

*Library of Congress Cataloging-in-Publication Data*
Deady, Kathleen W.
    Ancient Egypt / by Kathleen W. Deady.
      p. cm.—(Early civilizations)
    Includes bibliographical references and index.
    Contents: Discovering ancient Egypt—Early developments—Rise to
power—Struggles, rebuilding, and decline—Major achievements—
Evidence of Ancient Egypt.
      ISBN-13: 978-0-7368-2467-5 (hardcover)
      ISBN-10: 0-7368-2467-7 (hardcover)
      ISBN-13: 978-0-7368-4548-9 (softcover pbk.)
      ISBN-10: 0-7368-4548-8 (softcover pbk.)
      1. Egypt—Civilization—To 332 BC—Juvenile literature.
[1. Egypt—Civilization—To 332 BC.] I. Title. II. Series: Early
civilizations (Mankato, Minn.)
DT61.D357 2004
932—dc22                                                    2003014918

**Editor**

KATY KUDELA

**Designer**

KIA ADAMS

**Map Illustrator**

JOE LEMONNIER

**Photo Researchers**

SCOTT THOMS, KELLY GARVIN

**Product Planning Editor**

ERIC KUDALIS

# Table of Contents

*The Egyptian goddess Isis appears often in ancient Egyptian art.*

# CHAPTER 1

# Discovering Ancient Egypt

Nine-year-old Tutankhaten felt the heavy crown being placed on his head. His father King Akhenaton was dead. Tutankhaten would take his father's place. He would rule as king of Egypt. But he was a boy and knew little of being a king.

Tutankhaten needed help. He would depend on other peoples' advice to make important decisions. Like other kings, Tutankhaten believed he could do great things for his people and his country.

Tutankhaten did not grow old and become a great king. In fact, he only ruled for about nine years. During that time, his name was changed to Tutankhamun. He died suddenly in 1327 BC, at about 18 years old. Evidence from his mummy shows that he probably died from a fall or a hit on the head.

*Statue of King Tutankhamun* ➤

▲ Artists decorated King Tutankhamun's tomb with colorful wall paintings.

Like other kings of ancient Egypt, Tutankhamun was buried with his clothing, jewelry, and furniture. Ancient Egyptians believed he would need these things in his next life.

## A Peek at the Past

Almost 3,300 years passed since Tutankhamun's death. In 1922, **archaeologist** Howard Carter was digging in Egypt's Valley of the Kings. He was studying the rubble in this ancient burial ground.

♠ *Game boards were some of the many treasures found in King Tutankhamun's tomb.*

*Howard Carter's discovery of King Tutankhamun's mummy and tomb stirred excitement around the world. The young king's tomb had remained undiscovered for thousands of years.* ▼

Carter found stone steps that led to a blocked doorway. The door's seal read Tutankhamun. Behind the door were four small rooms. Thousands of gold items and jewels filled the rooms. A decorated gold coffin held the mummy of the Egyptian king.

Unlike other royal tombs of ancient Egypt, Tutankhamun's tomb was small. The small tomb was a clue that the king's death had been a surprise. The people probably did not have time to build a larger tomb.

Tutankhamun, or King Tut as he is often called, was not an important king. He is not remembered for being a great soldier or builder. But the discovery of his tomb and its **artifacts** made him famous. His tomb gave the world a view of ancient Egypt, a long lost **civilization**.

## An Advanced Civilization

The people of ancient Egypt had many new ideas. They were inventors. They studied math, science, **astronomy**, and medicine. They also created beautiful architecture, such as **pyramids** and **obelisks**.

Ancient Egypt was one of the oldest and greatest civilizations. For 3,000 years, it thrived along the banks of the Nile River in northeast Africa. Ancient Egypt helped human civilization develop.

*Ancient Egyptians made many advances in the areas of math and science. This water clock is just one tool the Egyptians used.* ➤

Ancient Egyptians combined their love of art with architecture. Today, historians are still amazed at Egyptian pyramids and obelisks. In 1838, artist Antonio Basoli painted this image of ancient Egypt. ▼

# CHAPTER 2

# Early Developments

Today, the land of northern Africa is mostly desert. The Nile River flows from east central Africa north to the Mediterranean Sea. At more than 4,100 miles (6,600 kilometers), the Nile is the longest river in the world. It is one of the few water sources in this hot, dry land. Thousands of years ago, the land was very different.

Long before 5000 BC, northern Africa was lush and green. The valley around the Nile River was much wetter. High flat plateaus of rich grassland and forests lay beyond the valley. The plateaus spread east to the Red Sea and west to the Atlantic Ocean. Plenty of rain fell, and many kinds of plants grew. Elephants, giraffes, and many other animals roamed the land.

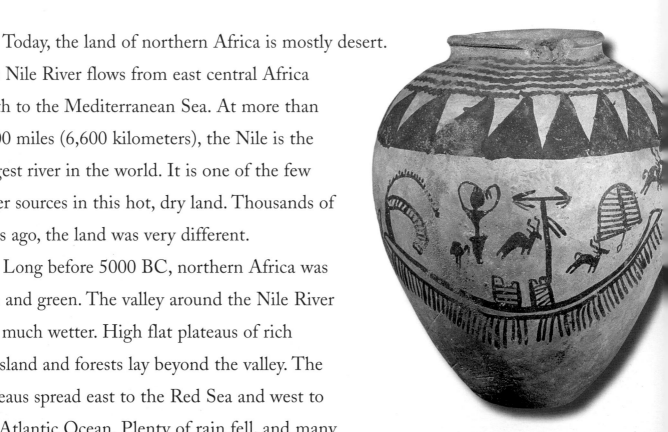

▲ *Art was a part of Egypt's earliest history. This pottery vase was created between 3300 and 2900 BC.*

Ancient Egyptians hunted and gathered food along the Nile River. This drawing is from a German publication dated 1881.

In ancient times, people lived mostly in the higher land outside the valley. They hunted animals for meat. They used tools like stone axes and bows and arrows. They picked fruits and berries from wild plants.

## Changes in Climate and Geography

Over hundreds of years, the climate began to change. The rainfall in central Africa decreased. Slowly, the grasslands dried into deserts.

With less rainfall, the water levels of the Nile fell. The water left rich soil deposits in the valley along the banks.

Little by little, animals moved down from the dry grassland plateaus into the river valley. The people followed the animals. The people moved into the valley near the flood plains along the river.

## Settlement and Advancements

Around 5000 BC, the people began to settle and build permanent homes. Slowly, they changed from food gatherers to food growers. They still hunted animals and fished in the river. They also kept cattle, sheep, and goats. They began to use these animals for wool and milk.

The people learned more about farming. They learned that vegetables and grains grew from seeds. They began scattering seeds in the rich soil of the river valley. They learned to make bread and weave linen from the **flax** they grew.

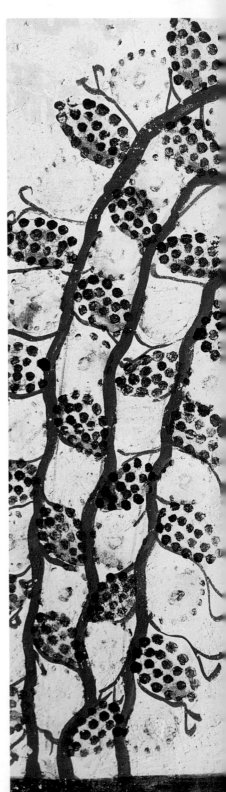

*The ancient Egyptians gathered wild berries and fruits, such as dates. This* v *painting was created betwe* 1400 and 1390 BC. ▼

Ancient Egyptians developed many skills. They made tools for farming. They made pottery, baskets, and stone carvings.

# Farming Along the Nile

Between June and September each year, the Nile overflowed its banks. Floods were common during the Shemu, or inundation, season. Heavy rains in central Africa and snow melting in the Ethiopian highlands caused this flooding.

The flooding season ended in October. Rich, black soil called silt was left behind on both sides of the river. This season was known as Peret, or sowing, season. During sowing season, farmers planted seeds.

From March to May, the farmers harvested their crops. They called the harvest season Akhet. The Egyptians harvested wheat, barley, fruits, and vegetables. Men, women, and children worked together. They had to finish before the annual floods came again in June.

## A Developing Civilization

The Egyptians began to organize. They learned a system of **irrigation** and managed the annual flooding of the Nile. Early settlements formed. As the settlements grew, leaders helped plan and organize the communities. Settlements grew into villages, and many villages grew into larger towns.

Life flourished along the Nile. Soon, Egyptians were building boats with oars. They traded with Nubia to the south. They also traded with Mesopotamia to the east across the Arabian Desert.

*The ancient Egyptians learned to farm the land. People worked together to plant and harvest the crops. This Egyptian drawing was created between 1306 and 1290 BC.* ▼

From around 3900 to 3100 BC, many villages grew into wealthy and powerful towns. Two areas formed into separate kingdoms. Upper Egypt developed in higher parts of the Nile Valley in the south. Lower Egypt grew in the north in the lower delta area.

Around 3100 BC, struggles between the two kingdoms broke out into war. King Narmer of Upper Egypt conquered Lower Egypt. He joined the two lands into one kingdom.

# CHAPTER 3

# Rise to Power

Historians believe the Egyptian civilization began with the joining of Upper and Lower Egypt. The union started a period of great growth and power for Egypt.

## The Early Dynastic Period

The Early Dynastic Period lasted about 450 years. This period was a time of great achievement. The most important achievement was a centralized system of government.

King Narmer built the center of Egypt's government in Memphis, near present-day Cairo. He was the first king of the First Egyptian **Dynasty**.

The Egyptian king, later called **pharaoh**, headed the government. His job was to watch over his kingdom. He protected the people.

Ancient Egyptians created this decorative piece of art, called the Palette of Narmer, around 3000 BC. Details from this stone artifact show King Narmer in battle.

The Egyptians believed their king was the god Horus in human form. They believed that he had the power to bring growth and wealth to the kingdom. This belief strengthened the king's power.

The king was an absolute ruler who made the laws. He did not have to obey the laws himself, but wise kings ruled justly. Priests served as the king's advisors. They held positions such as chief treasurer and army commander.

*The Egyptian sky god Horus was important to the people of ancient Egypt. They believed Horus took human form and came to Earth as their ruler. Horus also appeared as the figure of a hawk. This mural painting of Horus appears on an Egyptian tomb.* ▼

# Ancient Egypt's Dynasties

Ancient Egypt's history can be divided into seven major time periods. Egypt's earliest events took place during the Early Dynastic Period and the Old Kingdom. Other time periods that followed were the First Intermediate Period, the Middle Kingdom, the Second Intermediate Period, and the New Kingdom. Finally, the Late Period marked the end of Egyptian rule.

During Egypt's time periods, powerful leaders called kings ruled the land. More than 30 dynasties held power in ancient Egypt. King Narmer created Egypt's first dynasty.

In a dynasty, the king passed rule to the oldest son of his first wife. The king might also have several other, less important wives. Sometimes the main wife had only daughters. In a few cases, a daughter claimed the throne and ruled. Family dynasties ruled ancient Egypt for most of its history.

## Improvements

The central government organized society and improved life for the people. The government built a large irrigation system to bring river water to farm fields. During this time, Egyptians invented the ox-drawn plow. With plows, the farmers' work was easier. Farmers were able to grow more crops. These improvements helped Egyptian society develop.

An organized central government created a need for keeping records and accounts. By the time of the First Dynasty, the Egyptians had invented a system of writing. They wrote with signs called **hieroglyphics**. Using this language written in picture characters, Egyptians began keeping written records.

# Hieroglyphics and Scribes

Hieroglyphic writing was difficult to learn. The signs, like small pictures, could stand for one sound, more than one sound, a whole word, or an idea. Most Egyptians could not write hieroglyphs. Professional writers, called **scribes**, studied for years to learn more than 700 signs. Scribes were important to the kings. They were able to write tax and court records, as well as other important reports.

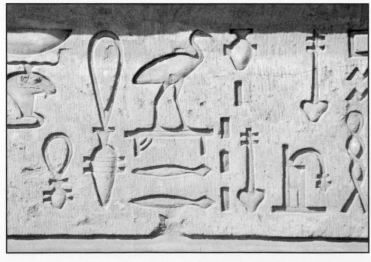

*Egyptian hieroglyphics* ♠

## Old Kingdom

Scribes kept written records for the king. This Egyptian wall painting shows scribes with reed pens. They are measuring and recording the kingdom's harvest. ▼

The Old Kingdom was a time of progress. The Third and Fourth Dynasties ruled during the Old Kingdom. The government was firmly established and towns grew. Egypt became wealthy and powerful. During this time, learning was important, and art thrived.

The Third Dynasty's second king, Djoser, had a chief scribe called Imhotep. Imhotep is best known as an architect. He built the Step Pyramid of Saqqara for King Djoser's tomb. This was one of the first stone buildings in the world.

The Egyptians later built even bigger pyramids. These pyramids were built for the tombs of other Old Kingdom rulers. The Old Kingdom is known as the Pyramid Age.

*The Step Pyramid of Saqqara was Egypt's first pyramid. This pyramid was built around 2780 BC.* ▼

King Snofru ruled during the Fourth Dynasty. During Snofru's rule, three pyramids were built. Snofru's son, King Khufu, later built the famous Great Pyramid for his father's tomb.

Two additional pyramids were built at Giza. The two pyramids were built for Khufu's son and grandson. A huge stone statue, called the Sphinx, guards the pyramids.

*The ancient Egyptians built the Sphinx to stand guard in front of the pyramids of Giza.* ➤

## Daily Life

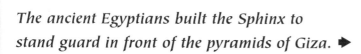

Families were an important part of everyday life in ancient Egypt. Children were welcomed and enjoyed. Families were often large.

Ancient Egyptians enjoyed parties with family and friends. They held dance and song festivals. Egyptians entertained friends at home with food and drink.

Egyptians enjoyed many pastimes. They liked fishing, swimming, and sailing on the Nile. Playing ball and wrestling were popular. People hunted crocodiles and hippopotamuses with bows and arrows and spears.

# CHAPTER 4

# Struggles, Rebuilding and Decline

King Pepi II ruled during the Sixth Dynasty. The rule of Pepi II was the longest in Egyptian history. Historians believe he ruled for about 94 years.

Toward the end of the Sixth Dynasty, local rulers and priests started fighting each other for power. The king's power weakened. Around 2134 BC, Egypt broke into separate states. These states lasted about 100 years. The Seventh to Tenth Dynasties are known as the First Intermediate Period.

Rulers during this period faced many troubles. People neglected the irrigation systems. Poor harvests caused a lack of food. People began to starve. Thieves broke into the pyramids for money.

The First Intermediate Period came to an end about 2040 BC. After years of struggle, the rulers in the southern city of Thebes united the kingdom again.

▲ *Ancient Egyptians filled a king's tomb with many valuable treasures. This jewelry storage chest was found in King Tutankhamun's tomb.*

*Thieves raided the tombs of ancient Egyptian kings for gold and other treasures.* ⬇

25

King Mentuhotep gained control of Egypt around 2040 BC. He moved the capital to Thebes, now called Luxor. With a strong central government, Egypt began to recover as the Middle Kingdom began.

## Middle Kingdom

Mentuhotep worked to rebuild the kingdom. He expanded the kingdom's territory. He traded with other countries. He also repaired and improved irrigation systems.

*Ancient Egyptians sailed to nearby countries to trade for goods.* ▼

# Growth of Ancient Egypt

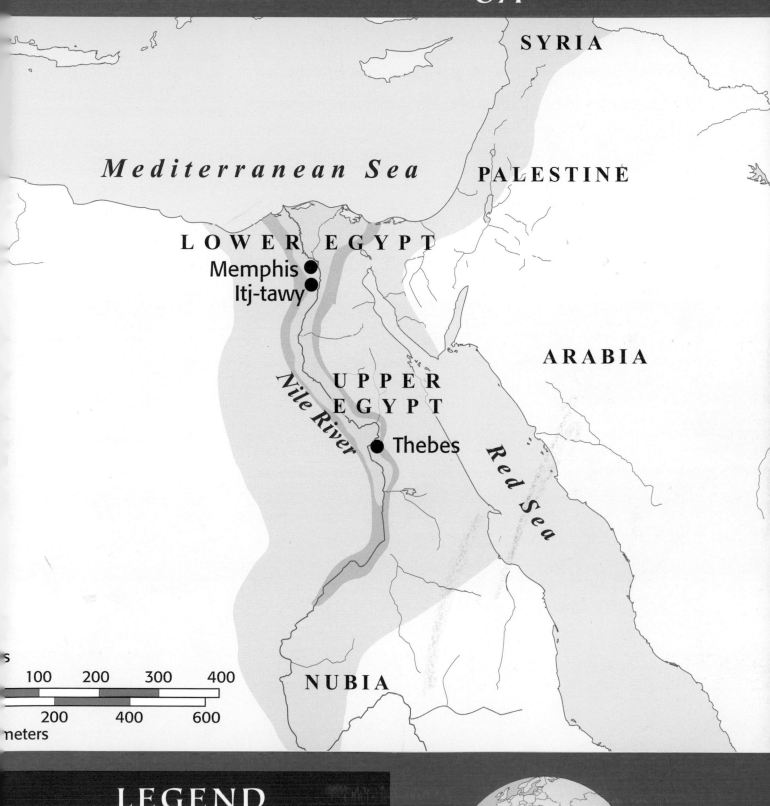

SYRIA

*Mediterranean Sea*

PALESTINE

LOWER EGYPT

Memphis

Itj-tawy

ARABIA

UPPER
EGYPT

*Nile River*

Thebes

*Red Sea*

100  200  300  400

200  400  600

meters

NUBIA

## LEGEND

Old Kingdom (2650–2134 BC)

Middle Kingdom (2040–1640 BC)

New Kingdom (1550–1070 BC)

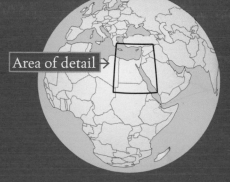

Area of detail →

In 1991 BC, a government official named Amenemhet took the throne and became king. King Amenemhet began the Twelfth Dynasty. He built a capital city named Itj-tawy near Memphis.

Under the rule of Amenemhet and rulers that followed him, Egypt became wealthy and powerful again. During this dynasty, Egypt again conquered Nubian territory and built up trade with Palestine and Syria.

*The Hyksos were fierce fighters. They used weapons made from bronze and iron. The Hyksos took control of Egypt around 1640 BC.* ▼

## Second Intermediate Period

Asian invaders, called Hyksos, came to Egypt around 1800 BC. As their numbers grew, so did their power. They took control around 1640 BC and lived in Lower Egypt. Hyksos kings ruled for about 100 years.

Around 1550 BC, the Egyptians finally defeated the Hyksos. General Ahmose drove the Hyksos out of Egypt. Ahmose became king. His rule began the New Kingdom.

## Weapons

During the Second Intermediate Period, Egyptians learned to make bronze weapons from the Hyksos. The Egyptians combined copper and tin using high heat. They used molds to shape the metal into arrowheads, spearheads, and battle-axes. Swords were invented as knife blades became longer and narrower. Later, the Egyptians made iron weapons.

The Hyksos also taught the Egyptians to make chariots. Horses pulled these two-wheeled carts. The chariot's wooden platform held two soldiers. The soldiers stood on the platform and fired their arrows.

*Egyptian daggers*

# New Kingdom

Under King Ahmose, the Egyptians worked so they would never be overrun again. Egypt developed from a peaceful kingdom into a military power.

Egypt set out to take control of other lands. They built a strong army. King Thutmose I used the army to fight and take control of land in Syria and Palestine.

Queen Hatshepsut also ruled during the 18th Dynasty. She ruled for about 21 years. Queen Hatshepsut was the longest ruling queen.

In the New Kingdom, Ramesses II ruled for more than 60 years. After 20 years of war with the Hittites in Syria, he made peace. He spent much of his later years building monuments.

# Late Period

At the end of the New Kingdom, Egypt's central rule grew weak. Pharaohs slowly lost control over lands outside Egypt.

At least 10 dynasties ruled Egypt over the next 700 years. By 712 BC, other people began moving into Egypt and gaining power. Rulers from Nubia, Assyria, and Persia formed many of the dynasties. Finally, Alexander the Great of Macedonia conquered Egypt in 332 BC.

▲ *An artist created this statue of Queen Hatsheps[u]t around 1504–1450 BC.*

*A naval battle called the Battle of Actium broke out between Rome and Egypt in 30 BC. At the end of this battle, the Roman Empire took control of Egypt.* ▼

For more than 300 years, Macedonian Greeks ruled Egypt. These people were the Ptolemies. The Ptolemies were descendants of Alexander's General Ptolemy. General Ptolemy ruled Egypt after Alexander's death. The last of the Greek line was Queen Cleopatra VII. She ruled with her two brothers and then her son Cesarion. He was the son of Julius Caesar of Rome.

About 37 BC, Cleopatra joined forces with Mark Antony, a Roman general. In 30 BC, the Romans defeated the Egyptian navy at the Battle of Actium. Egypt became part of the Roman Empire.

# CHAPTER 5

# Major Achievements

The pyramids are Egypt's best-known achievement. They are the oldest large stone structures in the world.

Building a pyramid was a huge task. Workers had to cut stone blocks from rock. First, they pounded wooden wedges into the rock. They wet the wedges, which made the wood swell. The swollen wood split the rock from the face of the **quarry**. Workers used copper chisels to smooth the block.

Slaves then dragged the blocks to barges. The barges floated down the Nile to the building site. Slaves hauled the stone blocks up ramps into place on the pyramid. They had to make the ramps longer and longer as the pyramid grew higher. Egyptians had no machines to help with the building. Teams of slaves took about 20 years to build one pyramid.

▲ *The pyramids of Giza are among ancient Egypt's greatest accomplishments.*

The ancient Egyptians worked carefully to build their pyramids. Exact measurements and the strength of many workers were needed to build the huge stone structures.

# Mathematics

Pyramids were built with planning and math. Egyptians learned to make exact measurements. Workers used barrels to help them measure length. Workers counted the number of times a barrel turned. They used the number of rolls as a measurement.

They also created a simple form of arithmetic. They began by counting their fingers. Counting was based on units of tens, hundreds, and thousands. Our decimal system today is based on early Egyptian methods.

# Calendar

Ancient Egyptians learned much about the geography of their land. From their knowledge, they developed a 365-day calendar.

The calendar was based on the annual flooding of the Nile River. The Egyptians learned the star Sirius rose once a year in the eastern sky just before dawn. They noticed each year that the Nile flooded just after the star appeared. This event became the starting date for their calendar. They then divided the calendar year into 12 months.

*Egyptian calendar* ➤

With their calendar, the Egyptians were able to date events when they recorded their history. These records have helped historians learn much about when things happened.

## Mummies and Medicine

To prepare a dead body for the next life, Egyptians learned how to keep it from rotting. They used a method called mummification. Only rich families could afford this treatment for their dead.

First, the Egyptians emptied the head and body cavity. They used a hook to remove the brain through the nose. They also cut open the body and removed the lungs, liver, and intestines. These organs were kept in separate containers, called **canopic jars**. They left the heart in the body.

Next, they washed the body with wine and spices. They packed the body in special salt to dry it out. They then stuffed the inside of the body with cloth to make it look fuller.

*Canopic jars were special containers used to hold the organs of a mummified body.* ➤

Finally, they oiled the body and wrapped it in strips of cloth. The body was put in a coffin. The whole process took about 70 days.

From mummification, the Egyptians learned many things about the inside of a body. They learned to set broken bones and treat wounds.

▼ *Ancient Egyptian mummy*

# CHAPTER 6

# Evidence of Ancient Egypt

The Egyptian civilization was one of the ancient world's most advanced. Egyptians left behind many facts of their history. Much of what historians know comes from studying this information.

## Learning about the Past

King Tutankhamun's tomb was an amazing discovery for archaeologists. This tomb was almost completely untouched for 3,300 years. When the tomb was opened, the contents gave the world a picture of the past.

Egyptians decorated the walls of their temples and tombs with beautiful artwork. These painted scenes tell of the lives of ancient Egyptians in great detail. The scenes also portray their dreams for their next life.

▲ *Today, the temple of Ramesses II stands as proof of ancient Egypt's advanced civilization.*

Egyptians left behind many written records. These records appear on the walls of temples and tombs, **papyrus** rolls, stone slabs, and pottery pieces. By AD 500, people no longer used hieroglyphics. They began to use a simpler alphabet that they learned from the Greeks. They quickly forgot how to read and write their ancient language. For centuries, hieroglyphics remained a mystery.

Then in 1799, someone found a rock slab outside the city of Rosetta, near Alexandria. The slab, called the Rosetta Stone, contained two forms of Egyptian writing and Greek writing.

Jean François Champollion, a French scholar, compared words he knew in Greek to words in hieroglyphics. Finally, in 1822, he figured out the hieroglyphics. The world could at last understand the hieroglyphics the ancient Egyptians had written.

*The discovery of the Rosetta Stone uncovered the mystery of ancient Egyptian hieroglyphics.* ➤

# Influences of Ancient Egypt

Ancient Egyptians influenced human development. They made advances in mathematics. Ancient Egyptians even influenced Western architecture. The ancient Egyptians' style can be seen in many buildings around the world.

*The Washington Monument in Washington, D.C., is designed like an Egyptian obelisk.* ▼

# TIME LINE

◆◆◆◆◆◆◆◆◆◆◆◆◆◆

**5000–3900 BC**

Early people settle around the Nile River, grow crops, and develop farming communities.

**3100 BC**

King Narmer unites Upper and Lower Egypt.

**2040 BC**

King Mentuhotep gains control of Egypt and moves the capital to Thebes.

**1640 BC**

Hyksos seize power and occupy Egypt until 1550.

BC   5000          3000          2000          1600

*Hunting scene*

**2134–2040 BC**

Egypt breaks into separate states.

*Battle of Actium*

## 1550 BC

General Ahmose drives the Hyksos from Egypt and becomes king; he begins Egypt's development as a military power.

## 332 BC

Alexander the Great from Macedonia conquers Egypt.

## 37 BC

Cleopatra joins forces with Roman general Mark Antony.

1500    1050    300    30

## 712–332 BC

Rulers from Nubia, Assyria, and Persia govern Egypt.

## 30 BC

Antony and Cleopatra are defeated at the Battle of Actium; Egypt becomes part of the Roman Empire.

# Famous People from Ancient Egypt

**Ahmose** drove the Hyksos out of Egypt about 1550 BC. He became king and established the 18th Dynasty and the New Kingdom.

**Cleopatra VII** was the last ruler of the Egyptian Empire. She ruled from 51 to 30 BC. She joined forces with Roman general Mark Antony. When Antony and Cleopatra were defeated by the Romans at the Battle of Actium, they killed themselves. Egypt became part of the Roman Empire.

**Djoser** ruled during the Old Kingdom. He was buried in the famous Step Pyramid. The Step Pyramid of Saqqara was one of the first stone buildings in the world.

**Hatshepsut** was the longest ruling queen in Egypt. Queen Hatshepsut ruled for 21 years. She ruled from 1490 to 1469 BC.

**Mentuhotep** gained control of Egypt, which began the Middle Kingdom. He moved the capital to Thebes. Mentuhotep gained control of Egypt around 2040 BC.

**Pepi II** had the longest reign as king in Egyptian history. Historians believe he reigned for about 94 years (2278–2184 BC).

**Ramesses II** ruled for more than 60 years (1290–1224 BC). He is known for building great monuments. Ramesses was the last great ruler before the start of Egypt's decline.

# Glossary

**archaeologist** (ar-kee-OL-uh-jist)—a person who studies old buildings, documents, and objects to learn about past life and activity

**artifact** (ART-uh-fakt)—an object made by human beings, especially a tool or weapon used in the past

**astronomy** (uh-STRON-uh-mee)—the study of stars, planets, and other objects in space

**canopic jar** (kuh-NO-pik JAR)—a jar in which the ancient Egyptians preserved the organs of a dead person

**civilization** (siv-i-luh-ZAY-shuhn)—an organized and highly developed society

**dynasty** (DYE-nuh-stee)—a series of rulers from the same family

**flax** (FLAKS)—a plant grown for its fiber and seed

**hieroglyphics** (hye-ur-uh-GLIF-iks)—Egyptian writing based on picture symbols that stand for a sound or word

**irrigation** (ihr-uh-GAY-shuhn)—a system of watering fields and crops by bringing water from a river through channels or pipes

**obelisk** (OB-uh-lisk)—a four-sided post of stone with a top shaped like a pyramid

**papyrus** (puh-PYE-ruhss)—a reed that grows along the Nile, especially in the delta; ancient Egyptians wrote on papyrus.

**pharaoh** (FAIR-oh)—another name for the Egyptian king

**pyramid** (PIHR-uh-mid)—a kind of tomb or burial building

**quarry** (KWOR-ee) a place where stone is dug from the ground

**scribe** (SKRIBE)—a professional writer in ancient Egypt trained to read and write hieroglyphics

**Ardagh, Philip.** *Ancient Egypt.* History Detectives. New York: P. Bedrick Books, 2000.

**Briscoe, Diana.** *King Tut: Tales from the Tomb.* High Five Reading. Mankato, Minn.: Capstone Curriculum, 2003.

**Kudalis, Eric.** *The Royal Mummies: Remains from Ancient Egypt.* Mummies. Mankato, Minn.: Capstone High-Interest Books, 2003.

**Steedman, Scott.** *The Egyptian News.* History News. Milwaukee: Gareth Stevens, 2000.

**Streissguth, Thomas.** *Life in Ancient Egypt.* The Way People Live. San Diego: Lucent Books, 2001.

# Internet Sites

FactHound offers a safe, fun way to find Internet sites related to this book. All of the sites on FactHound have been researched by our staff.

Here's how:

1. Visit *www.facthound.com*

2. Type in this special code **0736824677** for age appropriate sites.

   Or enter a search word related to this book for a more general search.

3. Click on the **Fetch It** button.

FactHound will fetch the best sites for you!

# Useful Addresses

**The British Museum**
Great Russell Street
London, WC1B 3DG
United Kingdom

The British Museum is known for its collection of Egyptian artifacts, such as mummies and sculptures. The museum's collection is the largest collection of ancient Egyptian artifacts outside of Cairo, Egypt.

**The Metropolitan Museum of Art**
1000 Fifth Avenue
New York, NY  10028-0198

Many of the artifacts displayed in this New York museum were discovered by the museum's own archaeologists. The museum's collection includes ancient Egyptian jewelry, statues, and architecture.

**Oriental Institute Museum**
1155 East 58th Street
Chicago, IL  60637

This Chicago museum has a collection of almost 30,000 Egyptian artifacts. Visitors learn about daily life and religion in ancient Egypt.

**Pyramids of Giza**
Ministry of Tourism Office
Misr Travel Tower, Abbassia Square
Cairo, Egypt

Today, visitors to Cairo, Egypt, can still see the magnificent pyramids built thousands of years ago. Standing guard in front of the pyramids is the Sphinx.

**Royal Ontario Museum**
100 Queen's Park
Toronto, ON  M5S 2C6
Canada

The Royal Ontario Museum's exhibit follows Egyptian history from 4000 BC to AD 324. Visitors to the museum will learn about pyramids, hieroglyphics, mummies, and much more.

◄ *Pyramids of Giza*

*Sphinx* ▼

# Index